YOUR **KINGDOM** COME

A STUDY FROM THE **HOLY LAND**

Copyright © 2018 by Beacon Hill Press of Kansas City
Beacon Hill Press of Kansas City
PO Box 419527
Kansas City, MO 64141
beaconhillbooks.com

978-0-8341-3690-8

Printed in the
United States of America

Cover design: Rob Monacelli
Interior design: Sharon Page

Published in cooperation with Trevecca Nazarene University.

The internet addresses, email addresses, and phone numbers in this book are ac-
curate at the time of publication. They are provided as a resource. Beacon Hill Press
of Kansas City does not endorse them or vouch for their content or permanence.

10 9 8 7 6 5 4 3 2 1

CONTENTS

INTRODUCTION

Thank you for being willing to guide the journey through *Your Kingdom Come!* This project grew out of a passionate curiosity to learn about the notion of kingdom in the Christian faith: Where did the concept of kingdom come from? How did it develop over time? What does it mean for us today?

Obviously the concept of kingdom is used many times in the Bible. If we look carefully, though, we can see that kingdom concepts developed in the hearts and minds of God's people across the ages. One of the central themes of Israel's history is that God is simultaneously attempting to make them into a kingdom while also trying to help them avoid becoming the kind of kingdom that is unfaithful to God's purposes.

This study, then, has a historical component. For those in your group who enjoy tracing historical trends and learning about how the biblical notion of kingdom fits into a larger historical picture, we have included some helps and guides that we think will be interesting. This study is also designed to be a spiritual journey. In the same way that God's people have been on a journey across the ages, we think your group could potentially join that journey and grow in faithfulness along the way. The discussion questions are meant to help you facilitate a conversation of exploration and discovery, not only of the way God has challenged God's people over time but also of how God is challenging us even now.

Each video is designed to introduce your group to the discussion that will follow. While the videos contain content that we hope will be helpful, we haven't designed them to be the centerpiece of the study. Rather, they serve as an orientation to open each session. We recommend allotting about ten minutes for the video, ten minutes to talk through the session with the group, and the remainder of the time dedicated to conversation around the provided questions. The sessions are short enough that participants can read through them prior to class and answer some of the reflection questions in advance if they wish.

These videos were filmed on location at various sites around the Holy Land. We chose sites with kingdom significance so you and your group can gain a better understanding of what it might have been like to live through the kingdom turning points in the history of God's people.

Our thanks to Trevecca Nazarene University's Department of Communication Studies for their commitment to this work, and especially to the dedicated group of students who comprised the film crew.

ABOUT THE CONTRIBUTORS

The lessons in this study were primarily written by religion and ministry students at Trevecca Nazarene University, who made the trip to Israel with us, were on location for the filming of each video segment, and conducted additional research to inform each lesson.

Dr. Timothy M. Green is the dean of the Millard Reed School of Theology and Christian Ministry at Trevecca Nazarene University. In addition to being a respected Old Testament scholar, he is also a sought-after speaker and teacher. His most recent publication is *The God Plot: Living with Holy Imagination,* available as a small group, video-based study from The Foundry Publishing.

Rev. Shawna Songer Gaines is the university chaplain at Trevecca Nazarene University. Her recent video-based, Bible study series called *Breathe* includes engaging and in-depth studies of the biblical themes of creation, wilderness, and exile. More information and video samples are available at breatheseries.com.

Dr. Timothy R. Gaines serves as assistant professor of religion at Trevecca Nazarene University. Together with Shawna Songer Gaines, he co-authored *Kings and Presidents: Politics and the Kingdom of God.* His most recent project, *Following Jesus: Prophet, Priest, King,* is a resource for those seeking to understand the promise and challenge of following Jesus in his prophetic, priestly, and kingly roles. Both are available from The Foundry Publishing.

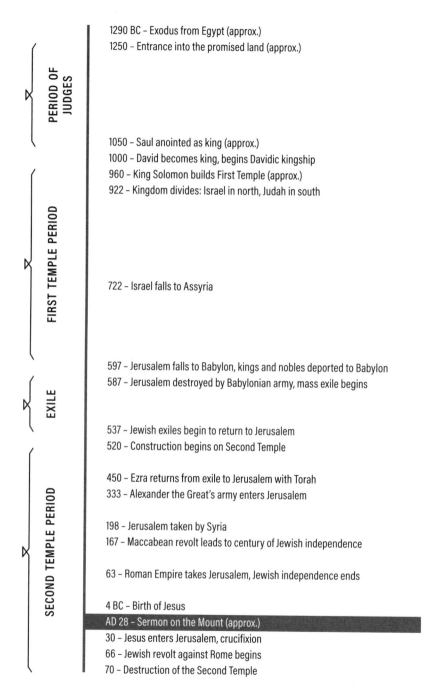

PERIOD OF JUDGES

1290 BC – Exodus from Egypt (approx.)
1250 – Entrance into the promised land (approx.)

FIRST TEMPLE PERIOD

1050 – Saul anointed as king (approx.)
1000 – David becomes king, begins Davidic kingship
960 – King Solomon builds First Temple (approx.)
922 – Kingdom divides: Israel in north, Judah in south

722 – Israel falls to Assyria

EXILE

597 – Jerusalem falls to Babylon, kings and nobles deported to Babylon
587 – Jerusalem destroyed by Babylonian army, mass exile begins

537 – Jewish exiles begin to return to Jerusalem
520 – Construction begins on Second Temple

SECOND TEMPLE PERIOD

450 – Ezra returns from exile to Jerusalem with Torah
333 – Alexander the Great's army enters Jerusalem

198 – Jerusalem taken by Syria
167 – Maccabean revolt leads to century of Jewish independence

63 – Roman Empire takes Jerusalem, Jewish independence ends

4 BC – Birth of Jesus
AD 28 – Sermon on the Mount (approx.)
30 – Jesus enters Jerusalem, crucifixion
66 – Jewish revolt against Rome begins
70 – Destruction of the Second Temple

SESSION 1

WHAT KIND OF KINGDOM?

J.J. Wyzinski

▼ HISTORICAL CONTEXT

Jerusalem and the surrounding area (modern Israel) were known as the land God had promised to Israel. Though Israel emerged as a kingdom as early as 1,200 years before Jesus, by the time Jesus was born, Jerusalem had been militarily overthrown by at least three foreign powers. During Jesus's lifetime, the Roman Empire came to power over Israel and established a political and military presence in Jerusalem. Though Rome did not force an end to Jewish worship, they also did not permit the people of Israel to govern themselves independently, and they regularly taxed the Jewish people to support Rome.

▼ LESSON

When Jesus was speaking to his followers about the kingdom of heaven in the Sermon on the Mount, he was using language they understood. A kingdom was a familiar concept in those days. Many of those who heard Jesus speak that day knew the stories of their ancestors, and how Israel had gone from being a group of slaves in Egypt to understanding itself as a kingdom. The hopes of their grandparents and great-grandparents had been that God would establish a way of life that would allow them to live as God's holy people. That meant that they needed real things like food, water, shelter, and freedom.

Whether it was Egypt, Rome, Babylon, Assyria, or any other kingdom that had taken power over them, the people gathered on that hillside listening to Jesus speak knew what these kingdoms were like. They were set up to funnel power to the ruler, often at the expense of the people. Any kingdom like that was not the kind of arrangement that would allow God's people to live according to their calling.

When Jesus came, he talked about a kind of kingdom that broke the mold from any kingdom these people had known before. Rather than give strength to the king, the kingdom Jesus preached about gave strength to those who were weak. Rather than being set up to conquer enemies, Jesus's kingdom was established on the basis of loving enemies (Matthew 5:43–48). The kingdoms the Israelites knew were about power and competition, but the kingdom Jesus offered was a way of life that allowed them to live as God's holy people. It was the surprising kind of kingdom their ancestors had prayed for. Not only that, but Jesus told them that this kingdom was near and that they were called into it now.

Jesus wasn't giving them a fantasy kingdom but a real one. Jesus called his followers to live in real ways according to the kingdom he was setting before them. The Lord's Prayer, as Jesus taught us to pray it, calls us not just to understand what his kingdom looks like but also to live its pattern in real-life ways, even now (Matthew 6:9–13).

▼ QUESTIONS FOR REFLECTION OR JOURNALING

1) Read Matthew 6:9–13. When we read the words, "Your kingdom come, your will be done, on earth as it is in heaven," what are we saying? What did Jesus intend for us to be praying with these words?

2) Why does Jesus still call us today to pray "your kingdom come"?

3) Read Matthew 5:1–11. What did Jesus mean when he said, "Blessed are the meek, for they will inherit the earth"? What does this mean for the kind of kingdom Jesus is bringing?

4) When Jesus said, "Blessed are the peacemakers, for they will be called children of God," what does that mean for those who wish to live in Jesus's kingdom?

5) What does the way of life look like that these Beatitudes call us to?

▼ VIDEO NOTES

▼ QUESTIONS FOR GROUP DISCUSSION

1) When you think of the word *kingdom,* what comes to mind? How is life structured for those who live in a kingdom?

2) Imagine the lives of those who heard Jesus preaching the Sermon on the Mount. They were ruled by a foreign king, and they were paying taxes to a foreign king. What do you think their hopes were for a new kingdom to be established?

3) How do you think the kingdom Jesus preached about was similar to or different from what they dreamed for themselves?

4) What kind of kingdom do you think Jesus is bringing today?

5) How might we, as a community, live now in this new kingdom?

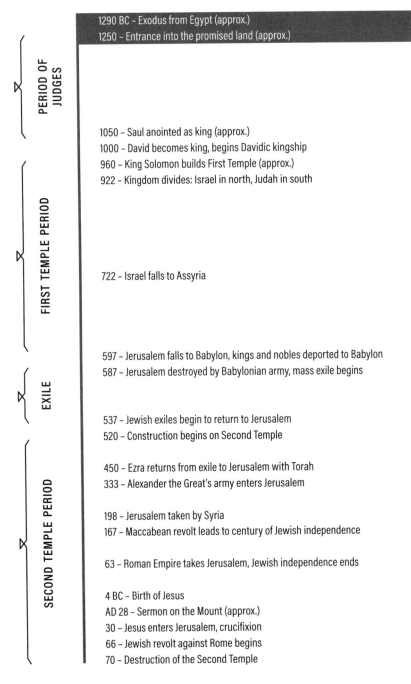

1290 BC – Exodus from Egypt (approx.)
1250 – Entrance into the promised land (approx.)

PERIOD OF JUDGES

1050 – Saul anointed as king (approx.)
1000 – David becomes king, begins Davidic kingship
960 – King Solomon builds First Temple (approx.)
922 – Kingdom divides: Israel in north, Judah in south

FIRST TEMPLE PERIOD

722 – Israel falls to Assyria

597 – Jerusalem falls to Babylon, kings and nobles deported to Babylon
587 – Jerusalem destroyed by Babylonian army, mass exile begins

EXILE

537 – Jewish exiles begin to return to Jerusalem
520 – Construction begins on Second Temple

450 – Ezra returns from exile to Jerusalem with Torah
333 – Alexander the Great's army enters Jerusalem

198 – Jerusalem taken by Syria
167 – Maccabean revolt leads to century of Jewish independence

63 – Roman Empire takes Jerusalem, Jewish independence ends

4 BC – Birth of Jesus
AD 28 – Sermon on the Mount (approx.)
30 – Jesus enters Jerusalem, crucifixion
66 – Jewish revolt against Rome begins
70 – Destruction of the Second Temple

SECOND TEMPLE PERIOD

SESSION 2

OUT OF THE WILDERNESS

Sabrina Phillips

▼ **HISTORICAL CONTEXT**

The forty years of wilderness wanderings after escaping slavery in Egypt mark a shift in the way God's people understood the concept of kingdom. For generations, they had come to trust in and rely upon Pharaoh's kingdom to provide their food, their shelter, and their security. But as long as they depended on Pharaoh's kingdom, they had to live according to the way of life in Pharaoh's kingdom. They could not live as God's holy people according to God's pattern; instead, they had to live as slaves in support of a king whose purposes were possessive and not redemptive. When they left Egypt, they left behind the way of life in Pharaoh's kingdom that prevented them from living according to God's pattern, but they also left behind the perks of a very powerful kingdom: food, water, safety, and security.

▼ **LESSON**

In contrast to the plentitude of Pharaoh's kingdom, the wilderness was hardly seen as a good place. The wilderness had no food, no water, and no military protection. This was a scary time for the people of Israel. But the wilderness wanderings were also a formational time because God began to create a new kind of kingdom imagination in God's people. Before God could form them into a kingdom, they needed to understand and trust that any kingdom with God in charge was going to be very different from Pharaoh's kingdom.

Freedom from slavery in Egypt meant that the people of Israel could finally live according to the patterns of God's kingdom, but it also meant they had to leave behind the patterns of Pharaoh's kingdom upon which they had come to depend. Perhaps that was why it took them forty years to be ready to enter the promised land. In those years, they came to trust in God's provision, rather than Pharaoh's. They came to understand that God's kingdom was not a kingdom like any they had known before. They came to know that God and Pharaoh ruled kingdoms in entirely different ways.

God used their wilderness wandering to deconstruct the way they understood what a kingdom was supposed to be so they could enter the promised land ready to be a people who would live according to the patterns of God's kingdom alone.

▼ QUESTIONS FOR REFLECTION OR JOURNALING

1) What are some of the differences between the kind of kingdom that Pharaoh ruled and the kind of kingdom into which God called God's people?

2) Read Exodus 16:1–3. Why were the people were talking like this as they began to enter the wilderness?

3) Compare the things the people of Israel did and said in the Exodus 16 passage to what they did and said in Joshua 1:1–9, 16–17. What do you notice is different about the Israelites from the time they began wandering in the wilderness to the time of this Joshua passage?

4) Read Joshua 3:7–17. What is happening in this passage as it relates to the people of God and their understanding of kingdom?

5) In the book of Acts, Stephen delivered a passionate speech before he was executed. In that speech, he encouraged those who heard him to join their lives to the kingdom God was establishing in Jesus. Read the portion of his speech recorded in Acts 7:35–40. What connections do you see between Stephen's speech and this lesson? Why did the people who heard Stephen have such a difficult time accepting his message?

▼ VIDEO NOTES

▼ QUESTIONS FOR GROUP DISCUSSION

1) Why did it take the people of God so long to adjust to the ways of God's kingdom?

2) How does the church today demonstrate its trust in earthly kingdoms while struggling to trust in the kingdom God is bringing?

3) In the 2017 publication *A Way Other than Our Own: Devotions for Lent,* Old Testament scholar Walter Brueggemann says, "The crisis in the U.S. church has almost nothing to do with being liberal or conservative; it has everything to do with giving up on faith and discipline of our Christian baptism and settling for a common, generic U.S. identity that is part patriotism, part consumerism, part violence, and part affluence." How does this quote help us answer this question: What is standing in the way of us being God's holy people?

4) Even in the wilderness, God still promises to provide for God's people. How has God provided for you this week?

5) How might we live courageously in God's kingdom this week?

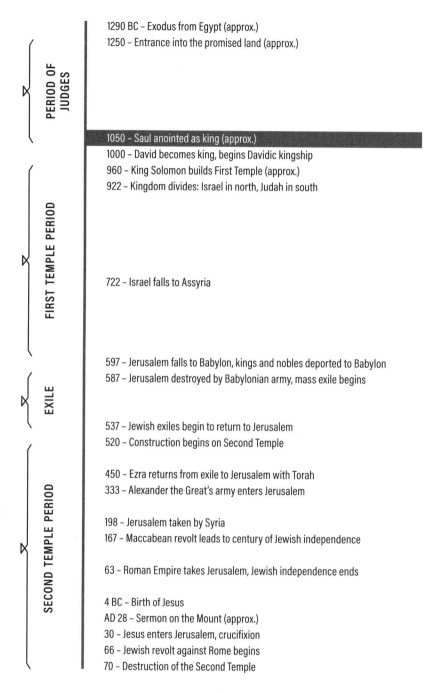

PERIOD OF JUDGES

1290 BC – Exodus from Egypt (approx.)
1250 – Entrance into the promised land (approx.)

1050 – Saul anointed as king (approx.)

FIRST TEMPLE PERIOD

1000 – David becomes king, begins Davidic kingship
960 – King Solomon builds First Temple (approx.)
922 – Kingdom divides: Israel in north, Judah in south

722 – Israel falls to Assyria

597 – Jerusalem falls to Babylon, kings and nobles deported to Babylon
587 – Jerusalem destroyed by Babylonian army, mass exile begins

EXILE

537 – Jewish exiles begin to return to Jerusalem
520 – Construction begins on Second Temple

450 – Ezra returns from exile to Jerusalem with Torah
333 – Alexander the Great's army enters Jerusalem

SECOND TEMPLE PERIOD

198 – Jerusalem taken by Syria
167 – Maccabean revolt leads to century of Jewish independence

63 – Roman Empire takes Jerusalem, Jewish independence ends

4 BC – Birth of Jesus
AD 28 – Sermon on the Mount (approx.)
30 – Jesus enters Jerusalem, crucifixion
66 – Jewish revolt against Rome begins
70 – Destruction of the Second Temple

SESSION 3

BUILD A PALACE OR BUILD A KINGDOM?

Justin Schoolcraft

▼ HISTORICAL CONTEXT

Another major turning point in the history of God's people took place when Israel eventually asked God for a king (1 Samuel 8), probably in response to the military incursions of foreign armies into Israel's territory. Around 1,000 BC, a governing structure of kingship began to form in Israel. Saul, an accomplished warrior, was the first to be named king of Israel, followed by David.

▼ LESSON

Until this point in their story, Israel had been a very different kind of nation, arranged not under a king who took but a God who gave. God had authorized the people to appoint judges who would help govern Israel, but from the time they entered the promised land until Saul was anointed, they lived in the land without a king.

Though asking for a king may not sound like a big deal to us, consider what a departure this was for Israel and what it signified—that they no longer trusted that the God who had rescued them from slavery, sustained them in the wilderness, protected them, and allowed them to live as a holy and distinct people, would continue to do so. They were doing more than merely asking for a king; they were abandoning the distinctive kind of existence that was capable of showing the world there was another way to be a kingdom. They stepped away from being the kind of people who demonstrated to the rest of the world that God could be trusted with their lives, their provision, and the political structure of their nation. They moved away from being a kingdom of priests and joined themselves to the pattern of every other kingdom that the world had ever seen.

The story recorded in the books of Deuteronomy through 2 Kings is a story of rise and fall. Israel corporately rose in power as they claimed land for themselves and built a temple for God to dwell in, but then they fell as the people turned to other, more convenient sources to sustain them. Moreover, on an individual level, judges and, later, kings rose in power and then fell according to whether they honored the life-giving ways of God.

At several points in Israel's history, exile was the result. God allowed them to be overtaken, a result of their turning away from their distinctive calling. Of course, exile was always meant to make them faithful to God once again, and the Lord sent prophets to call the people back to faithfulness and their distinctive way of being a kingdom. The underlying question throughout the narrative is simple: Why would the people turn away from the God who provides?

▼ QUESTIONS FOR REFLECTION OR JOURNALING

1) Read 1 Samuel 8:4–9. Why is God the rejected party and not
   Samuel?

2) How can we be tempted to turn to other methods of survival rather
   than trust God?

3) Read 2 Samuel 7:1–7. Why did David feel compelled to build a house for God?

4) Read Jeremiah 1:1–8, 11–13 and Jeremiah 31:31–34. How did Jeremiah, like other prophets, both acknowledge the sin of Israel and give hope for new life?

5) How can we speak prophetically to acknowledge sin but also re-
mind others of God's offer of new life?

▼ VIDEO NOTES

▼ QUESTIONS FOR GROUP DISCUSSION

1) What are the ways that the church can be tempted to box God in to a particular place?

2) Read 1 Samuel 8:10–20; 1 Kings 5:13–18; 1 Kings 11:1–10. What are the specific ways that Solomon fulfilled Samuel's warning of what kings would do?

3) Solomon is but one of many kings who turned from God. How can we encourage faithful leadership in the church today?

4) How do the people of God today struggle with the temptation to be like other peoples, adopting their ways of patterning life?

5) What have you learned about the relationship between the kind of people God asks us to be and the kind of people the world expects us to be?

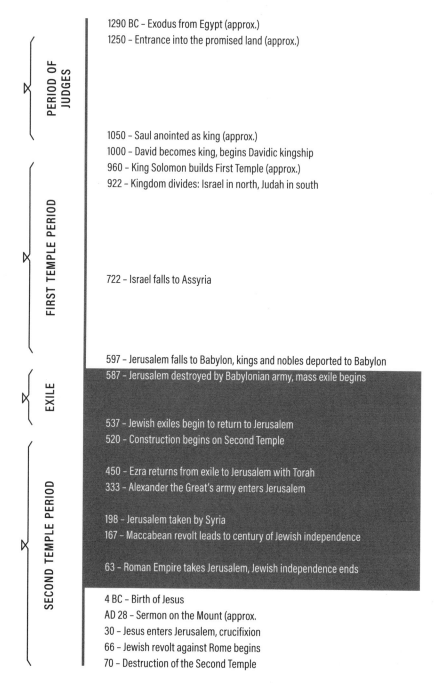

PERIOD OF JUDGES

1290 BC – Exodus from Egypt (approx.)
1250 – Entrance into the promised land (approx.)

FIRST TEMPLE PERIOD

1050 – Saul anointed as king (approx.)
1000 – David becomes king, begins Davidic kingship
960 – King Solomon builds First Temple (approx.)
922 – Kingdom divides: Israel in north, Judah in south

722 – Israel falls to Assyria

EXILE

597 – Jerusalem falls to Babylon, kings and nobles deported to Babylon
587 – Jerusalem destroyed by Babylonian army, mass exile begins

SECOND TEMPLE PERIOD

537 – Jewish exiles begin to return to Jerusalem
520 – Construction begins on Second Temple

450 – Ezra returns from exile to Jerusalem with Torah
333 – Alexander the Great's army enters Jerusalem

198 – Jerusalem taken by Syria
167 – Maccabean revolt leads to century of Jewish independence

63 – Roman Empire takes Jerusalem, Jewish independence ends

4 BC – Birth of Jesus
AD 28 – Sermon on the Mount (approx.
30 – Jesus enters Jerusalem, crucifixion
66 – Jewish revolt against Rome begins
70 – Destruction of the Second Temple

SESSION 4

FOUNDATION FOR A KINGDOM

Kathryn Schmelzenbach

▼ HISTORICAL CONTEXT

We come today to a point in Israel's history when they thought they had finally arrived as a kingdom. They had land, they had a king, they had an army, they had a temple—pretty much everything anyone would've needed to be one of the world's kingdoms. And that was precisely the problem: they had become one of the world's kingdoms, rather than a distinctive kingdom of priests under the reign of God. They began to look like all the other kingdoms of the world, and they even began to want to be like the other kingdoms of the world. So God stepped in and acted to preserve them as distinct. We refer to the result of that action today as exile. In 587 BC, the Babylonians over-threw Jerusalem, destroyed the temple, and carried away many of the Israelites as captives.

▼ LESSON

During their season of exile, the people of Israel began to hope their kingdom would one day be restored. Like the season of wandering in the wilderness, exile was an opportunity for them to come to desire the kind of kingdom God wanted them to be. When they were finally allowed to return to Jerusalem, the people of God had to reconstruct not only their homes but also their idea of kingdom. The Second Temple they built, to replace the one the Babylonians destroyed, never quite lived up to the glory of the First Temple. Nevertheless, Israel continued to hope that their kingdom would be fully restored, and over several generations, those hopes took several different forms.

The Sadducees hoped that aligning with the political rulers would restore the kingdom. The Pharisees hoped that setting themselves apart from the political rulers through distinctive dress and practice would usher in the kingdom. The Essenes withdrew into the caves and hoped for God to restore the kingdom while they devoted themselves to prayer and the study of Scripture. The Zealots hoped that violent revolt against political rulers would help God restore the kingdom.

Each of these hopeful responses grew out of what the adherents of these groups thought the kingdom was and what it should be. Eventually, a man from the Essenes—living, praying, and hoping in the wilderness—began to declare that the kingdom was drawing near in a way that would surprise everyone.

In our time, there are probably many different hopes for what kind of kingdom God will bring and how we should join God in bringing it. We must pay attention, however, to whether our hopes and expectations for the kingdom are faithful—because God may surprise us once more.

▼ QUESTIONS FOR REFLECTION OR JOURNALING

1) According to Jeremiah 23:1–8, why did the four different groups (Sadducees, Pharisees, Essenes, and Zealots) have different views on what the kingdom should look like?

2) How can people with the same basic background end up with such severely different views on kingdom?

3) How does the building of the foundation of the First Temple—and, later, the rebuilding of the new foundation for the Second Temple—relate to the people of God?

4) What different kinds of expectations do people have for the kingdom of God today?

5) What are your hopes for how God's kingdom will look?

▼ VIDEO NOTES

▼ QUESTIONS FOR GROUP DISCUSSION

1) Read Jeremiah 23:1–8. How does God keep God's promises for a kingdom?

2) Read Isaiah 11:11–12. How do these verses relate to Jeremiah 23:1–8?

3) When the people of God came out of exile, what kind of kingdom were they looking for?

4) What kinds of hopeful actions do you see in the church today of God's people preparing for God's kingdom to come on earth?

5) How do you think we can make faithful determinations about what kind of kingdom we should hope for and what we should do as we wait for it?

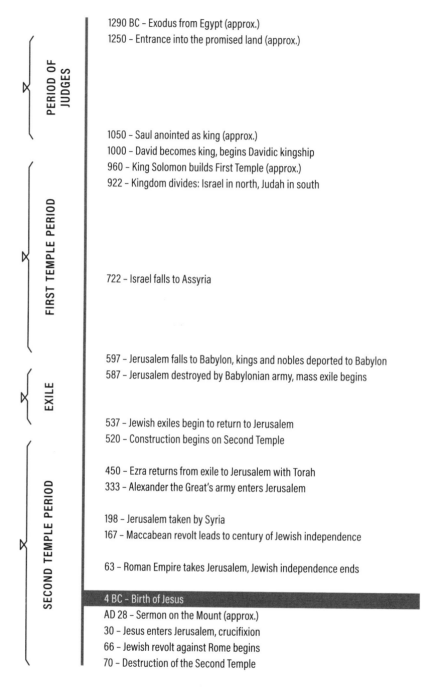

PERIOD OF JUDGES

1290 BC – Exodus from Egypt (approx.)
1250 – Entrance into the promised land (approx.)

FIRST TEMPLE PERIOD

1050 – Saul anointed as king (approx.)
1000 – David becomes king, begins Davidic kingship
960 – King Solomon builds First Temple (approx.)
922 – Kingdom divides: Israel in north, Judah in south

722 – Israel falls to Assyria

EXILE

597 – Jerusalem falls to Babylon, kings and nobles deported to Babylon
587 – Jerusalem destroyed by Babylonian army, mass exile begins

537 – Jewish exiles begin to return to Jerusalem
520 – Construction begins on Second Temple

SECOND TEMPLE PERIOD

450 – Ezra returns from exile to Jerusalem with Torah
333 – Alexander the Great's army enters Jerusalem

198 – Jerusalem taken by Syria
167 – Maccabean revolt leads to century of Jewish independence

63 – Roman Empire takes Jerusalem, Jewish independence ends

4 BC – Birth of Jesus

AD 28 – Sermon on the Mount (approx.)
30 – Jesus enters Jerusalem, crucifixion
66 – Jewish revolt against Rome begins
70 – Destruction of the Second Temple

SESSION 5

THE KINGDOM IS ARRIVING

J.J. Wyzinski

▼ HISTORICAL CONTEXT

At the time Jesus was born, the people of Israel were living in the land, but they did not have political control over the land. The Roman Empire had taken over Jerusalem, but they allowed the people of Israel to worship God as long as their worship did not interfere with the Roman kingdom. Caesar Augustus, who issued the order that took Mary and Joseph to Bethlehem, was the Roman political authority over the region of Judea. It was a common hope in those days that the Messiah would come and overthrow the Roman kingdom to establish a great and powerful Jewish kingdom that would be centered in Jerusalem.

▼ LESSON

If the kind of kingdom God is bringing seems a bit odd, consider God's history of establishing kingdom: God chose to begin the kingdom with an elderly, homeless man named Abraham (Genesis 17:4–6). And when God established a family lineage through which the kingdom would be built, God did so through David, the runt of his family (1 Samuel 16:1–13; 2 Samuel 7:1–17). Perhaps it should not surprise us, then, that when news of a king being born came to Israel, it was announced in the city of David, the unexpected runt king (Luke 2:1–4).

Odd news often gets announced in odd ways, and the birth of Jesus was no different. When God's kingdom was finally announced, it came to a group of shepherds at night (Luke 2:8–20) just a short distance from Jerusalem, the center of political power. The announcement did not come to those who were connected to power but to poor shepherds in a field.

The kingdom Jesus is bringing was not only announced to an unexpected group, but it also began to take root among unexpected people. From the beginning, Jesus talked about his ministry as one that would be for the poor and the oppressed (Luke 4:16–21). Perhaps that was why Jesus called a group of unlikely fishermen and other outcasts, rather than gathering the rising political stars of his day.

The oddest kind of kingdom came in the oddest kind of way among the oddest kinds of people. But isn't all of this consistent with the kind of kingdom God has wanted to bring from the beginning?

▼ QUESTIONS FOR REFLECTION OR JOURNALING

1) Read Luke 5:12–26. What do you see in this passage that helps shed more light on the kind of kingdom Jesus was establishing?

2) In Luke 5:27–32, Jesus called Levi. What was Jesus saying about the kingdom of God with his response to the Pharisees?

3) How does Jesus's response to the Pharisees in Luke 5:31–32 change the way we view the call to "fish for people"?

4) Through whom is God bringing God's kingdom?

5) What are the kinds of things you think we should do to join the kingdom that Jesus brought?

▼ VIDEO NOTES

▼ QUESTIONS FOR GROUP DISCUSSION

1) Read Luke 5:1–11. Why did Jesus go to a lake and not to a temple to call his followers?

2) When the disciples were shown just what Jesus was capable of in Luke 5:1–11, Peter was astounded and actually told Jesus to "go away." Why did Jesus continue to call Peter after this response?

3) We often see God teaching the disciples that their worthiness isn't a requirement in God's kingdom. How have we seen this play out in our own lives?

4) How is the kingdom Jesus brought still arriving in our world today?

5) What are some of the challenges we face as we seek to join the kingdom of God? Do you think we really want this kingdom today?

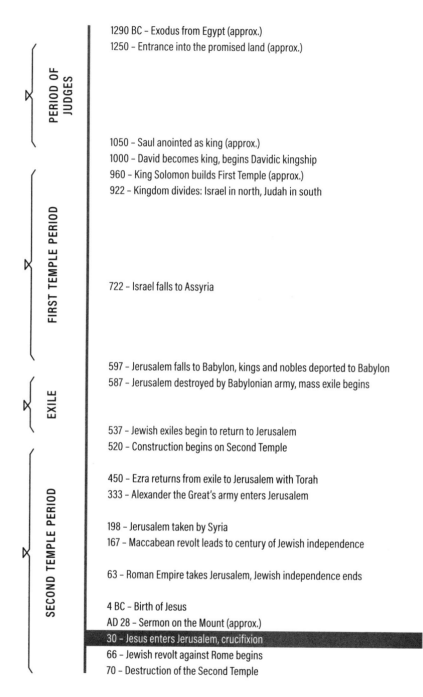

PERIOD OF JUDGES

1290 BC – Exodus from Egypt (approx.)
1250 – Entrance into the promised land (approx.)

FIRST TEMPLE PERIOD

1050 – Saul anointed as king (approx.)
1000 – David becomes king, begins Davidic kingship
960 – King Solomon builds First Temple (approx.)
922 – Kingdom divides: Israel in north, Judah in south

722 – Israel falls to Assyria

EXILE

597 – Jerusalem falls to Babylon, kings and nobles deported to Babylon
587 – Jerusalem destroyed by Babylonian army, mass exile begins

SECOND TEMPLE PERIOD

537 – Jewish exiles begin to return to Jerusalem
520 – Construction begins on Second Temple

450 – Ezra returns from exile to Jerusalem with Torah
333 – Alexander the Great's army enters Jerusalem

198 – Jerusalem taken by Syria
167 – Maccabean revolt leads to century of Jewish independence

63 – Roman Empire takes Jerusalem, Jewish independence ends

4 BC – Birth of Jesus
AD 28 – Sermon on the Mount (approx.)
30 – Jesus enters Jerusalem, crucifixion
66 – Jewish revolt against Rome begins
70 – Destruction of the Second Temple

THE KING AND HIS KINGDOM

Samuel Foster

▼ HISTORICAL CONTEXT

Nine hundred years before the birth of Jesus, Israel divided into two kingdoms. The northern kingdom was known as Israel while the southern kingdom was known as Judah. Jerusalem was located in Judah, about eighty miles from the northern region of Galilee, where Jesus spent much of his ministry. Galilee and Jerusalem are two distinctly different places.

Known for its bustling religious and political activity, Jerusalem was the cosmopolitan center of Jewish life. Galilee, on the other hand, was primarily known for its small fishing villages dotting the shores of the freshwater lake known as the Sea of Galilee. While residents of Jerusalem would have had access to many economic, intellectual, cultural, and educational opportunities, those living in Galilee—such as Jesus and his first disciples—would probably not have had access to the same opportunities.

▼ LESSON

Jesus's entry into Jerusalem is seen by many scholars as a type of kingly coronation—but in a strange and upside-down way. In some cultures, the way you are introduced carries a lot of weight. The way you are introduced cannot be duplicated, and it often leaves a distinct impression on those who may be meeting you for the first time. In the time of Jesus, kings who were being introduced wanted to make a bold statement, usually of power. This statement was meant to signify to the citizens of the region that the king was capable of undertaking the role of leadership. Why, then, did Jesus make such a strange introduction as he entered Jerusalem?

One would expect the king of the Jews to enter with an agenda of power and a statement of strength. However, Jesus entered in a way no king had done before: humbly. There was no agenda of self-promoting power but, rather, an agenda of self-giving love. There was no statement of threatening strength but one of steady hope.

This strange kind of introduction probably meant that few people in Jerusalem saw Jesus as a king upon his entrance. Many people likely saw what amounted to a silly and absurd spectacle: a group of folks making a commotion about a peasant carpenter from Galilee. How could a man like him be a king? He had no money, no army, no political connections—and he apparently had to borrow a donkey because he didn't even have a single horse to make his grand entrance! There were others, though, who began to see that Jesus was a different kind of king because he was bringing a different kind of kingdom. The Gospel writers try to help us understand that Jesus was bringing a kingdom very few people expected and that Jesus's kingdom challenges our expectations—even today.

▼ QUESTIONS FOR REFLECTION OR JOURNALING

1) Consider the most recent introduction of a king or political ruler that you have seen. Describe the kinds of things you saw as part of that event.

2) How does the kind of kingdom we see Jesus bringing challenge the way we tend to think about kingdoms today?

3) What kinds of kingdoms do we want, if we are honest? How are those kingdoms different from the kingdom Jesus brings?

4) Why do you think we may sometimes have trouble wanting the kind of kingdom Jesus is bringing? Why do you think we might have trouble trusting Jesus and the kingdom he is bringing?

5) What are some things we can do to align ourselves with the kind of kingdom Jesus is bringing and the kind of king Jesus is?

▼ **VIDEO NOTES**

▼ QUESTIONS FOR GROUP DISCUSSION

1) Read Luke 19:11–27. What does Luke tell us about why Jesus told this parable?

2) What characteristics of the king did you notice in this parable?

3) What kind of kingdom do you think the king in the parable ruled? What do you think that ruler or his kingdom valued?

4) Continue reading Luke 19:28–39. What do you notice about the way Jesus acts?

5) Why do you think Jesus tells the parable of the ruler just before entering Jerusalem? What differences can you see between the ruler in the parable and Jesus? What do you think this tells us about the kinds of kingdoms they each rule?

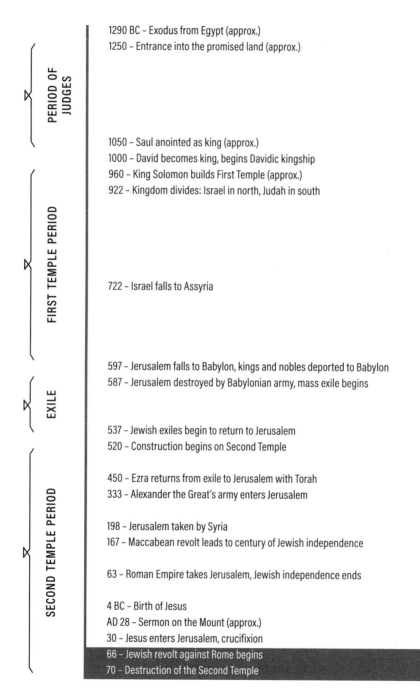

PERIOD OF JUDGES

1290 BC – Exodus from Egypt (approx.)
1250 – Entrance into the promised land (approx.)

1050 – Saul anointed as king (approx.)
1000 – David becomes king, begins Davidic kingship
960 – King Solomon builds First Temple (approx.)
922 – Kingdom divides: Israel in north, Judah in south

FIRST TEMPLE PERIOD

722 – Israel falls to Assyria

597 – Jerusalem falls to Babylon, kings and nobles deported to Babylon
587 – Jerusalem destroyed by Babylonian army, mass exile begins

EXILE

537 – Jewish exiles begin to return to Jerusalem
520 – Construction begins on Second Temple

450 – Ezra returns from exile to Jerusalem with Torah
333 – Alexander the Great's army enters Jerusalem

198 – Jerusalem taken by Syria
167 – Maccabean revolt leads to century of Jewish independence

SECOND TEMPLE PERIOD

63 – Roman Empire takes Jerusalem, Jewish independence ends

4 BC – Birth of Jesus
AD 28 – Sermon on the Mount (approx.)
30 – Jesus enters Jerusalem, crucifixion
66 – Jewish revolt against Rome begins
70 – Destruction of the Second Temple

SESSION 7

YOUR KINGDOM COME

Timothy R. Gaines

▼ HISTORICAL BACKGROUND

About thirty years after the crucifixion and resurrection of Jesus, an uprising began in and around Jerusalem. Jews began to rebel against Rome, the governing authority at the time, protesting the Roman Empire's ongoing taxation of the Jewish people. Hoping to overthrow the Roman Empire's political claim to Jerusalem, they eventually entered into armed conflict, attacking the Roman military garrison, which had been built very near the Second Temple. As part of that conflict, the temple was destroyed, sometime around 70 CE.

The consensus of most biblical scholars is that the Gospel of Matthew was written within a few years of that uprising. Perhaps that is part of the reason Matthew features the Sermon on the Mount so prominently in the opening chapters of his Gospel. There, the words of Jesus offer a distinctly different kind of kingdom than that of the Roman Empire, or even the kind of kingdom Jewish rebels were attempting to defend in Jerusalem.

▼ LESSON

The people who gathered on the hill above the Sea of Galilee to hear Jesus teach had been waiting for the kingdom their whole lives. They knew the stories of their ancestors, who had also been waiting for God to establish a kingdom. In what we have seen over the course of this study, the people of Israel had been talking about kingdom for a very, very long time. Their hopes for a kingdom had been shaped over generations, from becoming dependent upon Pharaoh's kingdom while they were slaves to having God use the wilderness season to reshape their imaginations for a kingdom in which God alone would be their Lord.

God gave them the land, and they entered as a very different kingdom, depending on God alone for their protection and provision. In only a few short generations, they were comparing themselves to the nations around them and asking God to give them a king. When their kings began to act in ways that were similar to the kings of all the other nations, God used a season of exile to help reset their kingdom imagination. With Jesus, God was doing something new: becoming flesh and establishing the kingdom among them.

The kingdom Jesus brought was a spiritual reality, but it was not *only* spiritual. It had flesh-and-blood consequences. It called the disciples to get involved and to live their lives in accordance with Jesus's proclaimed kingdom. Yes, sometimes that meant it put them at odds with the other kingdoms of the world, but if there was nothing different about the way they were living their lives, what good would they be to anyone else?

One day, God will renew all of creation. The old will pass away, and everything will become new. But until that time, God is calling those who follow Jesus to live according to the very real, very here-and-now kingdom that a carpenter from Nazareth initiated when he turned to a crowd of kingdom-curious folks on a hillside in Galilee and began to say, "Blessed are the poor in spirit, for theirs is the kingdom of heaven."

▼ QUESTIONS FOR REFLECTION OR JOURNALING

1) What challenges do you think face those who seek to live in the kingdom Jesus is bringing?

2) What are the best things we can do to remain faithful to the kingdom Jesus is bringing, even in the face of challenges?

3) Read Matthew 6:9–13. What echoes of Israel's hopes for a kingdom do you hear in this prayer?

4) Take a moment to talk through each line of the Lord's Prayer in Matthew 6. If the citizens of Jesus's kingdom earnestly prayed this prayer, what do you think that would do to the way they live their lives?

5) Reflecting back over the past several sessions of this study, what have you learned about Israel's expectations for kingdom? How might that apply to our expectations for kingdom?

▼ VIDEO NOTES

▼ QUESTIONS FOR GROUP DISCUSSION

1) Read Matthew 5:1–48 together. List the things that stand out to you as you hear this read aloud. What kind of kingdom do you think Jesus is establishing?

2) Remember back to Pharaoh's kingdom in Egypt. What are the main differences you see between his kingdom and the kingdom Jesus is talking about in this passage?

3) Based on what you've just read, what do you think the life of the ideal citizen of the kingdom of Jesus looks like? How does he or she live? What does he or she do?

4) Take a moment to talk about the kingdom expectations we experience today. What kind of kingdom do you think Christians want to be established? Do you think it is like the kingdom Jesus is establishing?

5) Spend a few minutes in prayer, asking God to provide a clear vision of the kingdom Jesus has brought and the strength to live faithfully to that kingdom. Close by praying the Lord's Prayer together.